The Narcissistic Parent:

A Guidebook for Legal Professionals Working with Families in High-Conflict Divorce

C.A. Childress, Psy.D.

Oaksong Press

The Narcissistic Parent: A Guidebook for Legal Professionals
Working with Families in High-Conflict Divorce

Oaksong Press. Claremont, California

Copyright © 2016 Craig Childress

Printed in the United States of America
ISBN 978-0-9961145-4-7

Contents

Introduction   1

The Narcissistic Parent   4

A Hidden Pathology   6

Blame and Projection   8

Triangulation of the Child   12

Disregard for Truth and Authority   19

Trauma Reenactment Narrative   23

Processing Sadness and Grief   26

The Co-Narcissistic Child   28

The Attachment System   31

Child Testimony   34

Epilogue: The Dark Triad   38

References   41

Introduction

This booklet is designed to help legal professionals more effectively recognize the pathology of a narcissistic parent in high-conflict divorce. Mental health professionals who interface regularly with the legal system are required by professional practice standards to understand basic legal procedures so that they can effectively perform their mental health roles within the context of the legal system. In a similar way, legal professionals who interface regularly with the mental health system, such as minor's counsel, guardians ad litem, and family law judiciary, need to have a fundamental understanding for parental personality disorder pathology that can be a contributing factor to the high-conflict court cases under their consideration.

Narcissistic and borderline personality parents are among the worst parents possible, and their severely poor parenting can rise to the level of psychological child abuse. The outward appearance of this severely pathological parent-child relationship, however, may be one of hyper-bonded closeness (called "psychological enmeshment") which represents a pathological role-reversal relationship in which the child's psychological integrity is violated and used (manipulated and exploited) to meet the emotional and psychological needs of the parent. Yet because of the superficial outward appearance of parent-child bonding (i.e., the role-reversal relationship in which the child is responding in ways to meet the parent's needs), the narcissistic pathology of the parent can elude recognition by many legal professionals who will misinterpret the psychological enmeshment as an indication of healthy parent-child bonding. Psychological enmeshment is <u>not</u> a healthy relationship.

The role-reversal pathology with a narcissistic parent is extremely pathological. It essentially involves the parent psychologically feeding off of the child's self-structure development in order to support the inadequate self-structure of the parent. Yet despite the severity of the pathology, even many mental health professionals who are inexperienced with assessing narcissistic pathology will incorrectly interpret the outward appearance of the hyper-affectionate and over-involved parent-child relationship as evidence of parent-child bonding rather than enmeshed psychopathology. When this occurs, the naivety and inexperience of these legal and mental health professionals will become captivated by the superficial charm and seemingly rational self-assertive presentation of the narcissistic personality and become allies in enacting the pathology within the family.

The severe psychopathology of the narcissistic personality only becomes evident under certain select circumstances, otherwise its external appearance is one of calm self-assurance. The narcissistic personality is particularly vulnerable to psychological collapse in response to rejection. Divorce represents exactly the sort of rejection by the spousal attachment figure that will trigger a narcissistic collapse into intense anger and an obsessive need to seek revenge.

The narcissistic personality is extremely manipulative and exploitative, and the narcissistic parent will readily incorporate the child into the spousal conflict as a means of enacting a cruel revenge on the other spouse for the narcissistic injury of the divorce. By forcing the child to choose sides in the spousal conflict, the narcissistic parent exploits the child as a tool, as a weapon, to be used in the spousal conflict with the other parent. The narcissistic parent "triangulates" the child into the spousal conflict as a means of stabilizing the collapsing personality structure of the narcissistic parent that has been challenged by the rejection of the divorce.

When the narcissistic parent forces the child to choose sides in the spousal conflict, the child's only escape from being caught in the middle of the spousal conflict is to align with the narcissistic parent against the other parent. If the child tries to maintain a bonded relationship with the other parent, or even tries to remain neutral in the spousal conflict, then the narcissistic parent will continually place the child directly in the middle of the ongoing spousal conflict to create as much psychological stress for the child as possible. The narcissistic parent will continually force the child through manipulative communications into choosing a side in the spousal conflict. The only escape for the child from the psychological stress of continually being placed in the middle of the spousal conflict by the pathology of the narcissistic parent is for the child to align with the narcissistic parent against the other parent (called a "cross-generational coalition").

In the world of the narcissistic parent, truth and reality are malleable constructs that can change based on the moment-to-moment emotional and psychological needs of the parent. In this context of arbitrarily defined reality, the child must continually monitor the state of the narcissistic parent in order to respond in ways that keep the narcissistic parent in an organized and regulated emotional and psychological state. Eventually, the child's "regulatory object" function for the narcissistic parent requires that the child psychologically surrender to the reality constructed by the parent. In response to the psychologically "invalidating environment" created by the needs of the narcissistic parent, the child's own self-authenticity is eventually sacrificed to the arbitrary definition of reality created by the narcissistic parent.

The following introductory primer on the narcissistic parent relies on descriptions of narcissistic pathology drawn directly from the professional literature to highlight the various features of the narcissistic parent's pathology, their psychological control of the child, and the role-reversal relationship that the narcissistic parent creates with the child in order to meet the emotional and psychological needs of the parent. High-conflict divorce always entails at least one narcissistic parent, because normal-range parents will limit their inter-spousal conflict out of concern for the child's well-being and empathy for the child's needs. A narcissistic parent, however, will intentionally create continual conflict within the family and will purposely draw the child into the inter-spousal conflict as a means to meet the emotional and psychological needs of the narcissistic parent.

The failure by legal professionals to recognize the severe psychopathology of the narcissistic parent as it is being enacted in the family's relationships can result in the manipulation and exploitation of these legal professionals by the narcissistic parent into becoming allies who collude with the enactment of the psychopathology in the family, to the severe developmental, emotional, and psychological detriment of the child.

The Narcissistic Parent

Parental empathy for the child's authentic experience is the single most important parental quality necessary for healthy child development. Conversely, research indicates that the absence of parental empathy is at the root of child abuse:

> "The act of child abuse by parents is viewed in itself as an outgrowth of parental failure of empathy and a narcissistic stance towards one's own children. Deficiency of empathic responsiveness prevents such self-centered parents from comprehending the impact of their acts, and in combination with their fragility and need for self-stabilization, predisposes them to exploit children in this way." (Moor & Silvern, 2006, p. 95)

> "Only insofar as parents fail in their capacity for empathic attunement and responsiveness can they objectify their children, consider them narcissistic extensions of themselves, and abuse them. It is the parents' view of their children as vehicles for satisfaction of their own needs, accompanied by the simultaneous disregard for those of the child, that make the victimization possible." (Moor & Silvern, 2006, p. 104)

The absence of empathy is a defining characteristic of the narcissistic parent. The narcissistic personality:

> "Lacks empathy: is unwilling to recognize or identify with the feelings and needs of others." (DSM-5 Diagnostic Criteria 7; American Psychiatric Association, 2013, p. 670)

Instead, the narcissistic parent exploits the child to meet the parent's own emotional and psychological needs:

> "Is interpersonally exploitative, i.e., takes advantage of others to achieve his or her own ends." (DSM-5 Diagnostic Criteria 6; American Psychiatric Association, 2013, p. 670)

"Narcissistic parents are seen as treating their children as extensions of themselves, expecting them to meet their own narcissistic needs, as unable to meet their children's needs for acceptance, as critical and angry when their children try to express their own feelings, will, and independent personality; and as obstructing the development of their children's true self." (Cohen, 1998, p. 199).

"The need to *control* the idealized objects, to use them in attempts to manipulate and exploit the environment and to "destroy potential enemies," is linked with inordinate pride in the "possession" of these perfect objects totally dedicated to the patient." (Kernberg, 1975, p. 33)

The narcissistic and borderline personality parent (which are external variants of the same underlying core pathology) are among the worst parents possible. A potential rank ordering of the worst possible parents would be the following:

1. Sexually abusive parent – incest;

2. Narcissistic and borderline personality parent;

3. Physically abusive parent;

4. Extreme parental neglect;

5. Parental mental illness (e.g., untreated schizophrenia, untreated bipolar disorder, untreated major depression).[1]

Mental health professionals may disagree slightly about the exact order of which parental pathology is worse for the child, but narcissistic and borderline parents are nevertheless among the worst possible parents. It is incumbent upon all legal professionals whose roles interface with possible mental health pathology within the family (e.g., minor's counsel, guardians ad litem, and family law judiciary) to be professionally familiar with the characteristic expression of parental narcissistic pathology within the family in order to enact their role in protecting the healthy emotional and psychological development of children.

---

[1] Mental illness that is properly treated and stabilized with medication and therapy presents considerably reduced clinical concerns surrounding parental capacity.

A Hidden Pathology

Narcissistic personality traits are not easily recognized and can frequently be overlooked, even by mental health professionals who are often untrained and inexperienced in diagnosing personality disorder pathology in a family context (such as individual child therapists):

> "While narcissism is recognized as a serious mental disorder, its manifestations may not be immediately recognized as pathological, even by persons in the helping professions, and its implications may remain unattended to." (Cohen, 1998, p. 197)

The reason that narcissistic personality pathology often goes unrecognized is that the narcissistic personality presents well in superficial social contexts and the extent of the pathology only becomes evident under select circumstances:

> "The perception [of narcissism] is hampered by the fact that narcissistic individuals may well be intelligent, charming, and sometimes creative people who function effectively in their professional lives and in a range of social situations." (Cohen, 1998, p. 197)

> "When not faced with humiliating or stressful situations, CENs [Confident-Egoistic-Narcissistic] convey a calm and self-assured quality in their social behavior. Their untroubled and self-satisfied air is viewed by some as a sign of confident equanimity." (Millon, 2011, p. 388-389)

> "Narcissists can display a deceptively warm demeanor." (Beck et al., 2004, p. 241)

> "The core belief of narcissistic personality disorder is one of inferiority or unimportance. This belief is only activated under certain circumstances and thus may be observed mainly in response to conditions of self-esteem threat. Otherwise, the

manifest belief is a compensatory attitude of superiority." (Beck et al., 2004, p. 249)

"Highly intelligent patients with this personality structure may appear as quite creative in their fields: narcissistic personalities can often be found as leaders in industrial organizations or academic institutions; they may also be outstanding performers in some artistic domain." (Kernberg, 1977, p. 229)

The narcissistic personality rarely presents for therapy, so most mental health professionals seldom have the opportunity to see this severe form of personality pathology. Their lack of clinical experience in assessing and diagnosing this form of pathology contributes to their inability to recognize parental narcissistic pathology when it presents in their practice.

The narcissistic personality uses superficial charm and confident self-assertion to enlist allies. Mental health and legal professionals who are not experienced in recognizing the narcissistic personality are highly vulnerable to becoming allies in the psychological manipulation and exploitation of the child by the narcissistic parent, who nullifies the child's self-authenticity to meet the emotional and psychological needs of the narcissistic parent.

"To the extent that parents are narcissistic, they are controlling, blaming, self-absorbed, intolerant of others' views, unaware of their children's needs and of the effects of their behavior on their children, and require that the children see them as the parents wish to be seen. They may also demand certain behavior from their children because they see the children as extensions of themselves, and need the children to represent them in the world in ways that meet the parents' emotional needs." (Rappoport, 2005, p. 2)

"In a narcissistic encounter, there is, psychologically, only one person present. The co-narcissist disappears for both people, and only the narcissistic person's experience is important." (Rappoport, 2005, p. 2)

Blame & Projection

One of the most prominent features of the narcissistic personality is externalizing blame onto others:

"The propensity to blame is an outstanding feature... of narcissistic behavior in general. It is a way for the narcissist to see himself in a good light and a manifestation of the splitting off of the negative aspects of the self and projecting them onto others that is a major narcissistic defense." (Cohen, 1998, p. 206)

"He or she [the narcissist] remains firmly rooted in the importance of a flawless or powerful image... Without a flawless image, core beliefs of inferiority become activated." (Beck et al., 2004, p. 246)

"If others fail to satisfy the narcissist's "needs," including the need to look good, or be free from inconvenience, then others "deserve to be punished"... Even when punishing others out of intolerance or entitlement, the narcissist sees this as "a lesson they need, for their own good." (Beck et al., 2004, p. 252)

Blaming others for failures and inadequacies in order to maintain the desired narcissistic self-image of grandiose self-perfection is the product of two psychological processes characteristic of the narcissistic personality, *splitting* - in which people are seen in polarized extremes of all-good and all-bad; and *projection* – in which unacceptable personal qualities are psychologically expelled and placed on other people:

"The narcissist exaggerates his own importance, achievements, abilities, talents, and efforts, while splitting off, disassociating, or repressing negative elements of his self and projecting them onto others." (Cohen 1998, p. 198)

"Narcissist persons eliminate bad aspects of themselves using massive projections. Naturally, such projections contaminate external objects that are then experienced as "dangerous, threatening, and worthless." (Svrakic, 1990, p. 193)

"The normal tension between actual self on the one hand, and ideal self and ideal object on the other, is eliminated by the building up of an inflated self concept within which the actual self and the ideal self and ideal object are confused. At the same time, the remnants of the unacceptable self images are repressed and projected onto external objects which are devalued." (Kernberg, 1975, p. 217)

"The motivation of selfishness predominates in the minds of narcissistic people. It is a major component of their defensive style, and it is therefore a motivation they readily attribute to (or project onto) others." (Rappoport, 2005, p. 3)

Both *splitting* and *projection* are considered very primitive psychological defenses. Splitting is revealed through a lack of ambivalence. The psychological defense of splitting entails polarized perceptions in extremes of all-good and all-bad. The American Psychiatric Association defines splitting as:

"The individual deals with emotional conflict or internal or external stressors by compartmentalizing opposite affect states and failing to integrate the positive and negative qualities of self or others into cohesive images. Because ambivalent affects cannot be experienced simultaneously, more balanced views and expectations of self or others are excluded from emotional awareness. Self and object images tend to alternate between polar opposites; exclusively loving, powerful, worthy, nurturant, and kind – or exclusively bad, hateful, angry, destructive, rejecting, or worthless." (American Psychiatric Association, 2000, p. 812)

Projection is defined by the American Psychiatric Association as:

"The individual deals with emotional conflict or internal or external stressors by falsely attributing to another his or her own unacceptable feelings, impulses, or thoughts." (American Psychiatric Association, 2000, p. 812)

The Term "Abusive"

Use of the terms "abuse" or "abusive" to characterize another person's actions are frequently diagnostic of one of two possible alternatives:

A.) Authentic abuse;

B.) Splitting pathology involving polarization of perception into extreme attitudes.

If authentic abuse is **not** present yet the term "abusive" is being used by one parent to describe the other spouse-and-parent, then this is often the product of *splitting,* in which the actions of the other spouse-and-parent are perceived through the *splitting* pathology of the narcissistic parent in extremes of all-good or all-bad rather than in more balanced and realistic terms. Normal people tend to use less inflammatory terms to describe the undesirable actions of others, such as inconsiderate, rude, inflexible, mean, horrible, nasty, but rarely "abusive," because normal-range people recognize the extreme nature of the term "abuse." To accuse someone of being "abusive" is a serious allegation that immediately elicits a protective response from others. The splitting pathology, however, perceives other people in <u>extremes</u> of all-good or all-bad and will therefore frequently characterize the undesired behavior of others in extreme terms such as "abusive" in order to manipulatively exploit the protective response this allegation receives from others.

At a psychological level, it is the narcissistic parent who is manipulating and exploiting the child through a role-reversal relationship that meets the parent's needs while violating the child's psychological integrity. The allegation of "abusive" parenting made by a narcissistic parent toward the other parent often also represents a self-accusatory *projection* of the narcissistic parent's own psychologically abusive relationship with the child:

"The act of child abuse by parents is viewed in itself as an outgrowth of parental failure of empathy and a narcissistic stance towards one's own children. Deficiency of empathic responsiveness prevents such self-centered parents from comprehending the impact of their acts, and in combination with their fragility and need for self-stabilization, predisposes them to exploit children in this way." (Moor & Silvern, 2006, p. 95)

"Only insofar as parents fail in their capacity for empathic attunement and responsiveness can they objectify their children, consider them narcissistic extensions of themselves, and abuse them. It is the parents' view of their children as vehicles for satisfaction of their own needs, accompanied by the simultaneous disregard for those of the child, that make the victimization possible." (Moor & Silvern, 2006, p. 104)

With the caveat that authentic abuse should <u>always</u> be considered whenever there is an allegation of child abuse, a differential diagnosis of *splitting* and *projection* should also be considered when authentic abuse is <u>not</u> present yet the term "abusive" is used to characterize the actions of the other spouse.

Projection

Projection is one of the primary psychological defenses of the narcissistic personality. The narcissistic personality rejects his or her own feelings of self-inadequacy and instead projects these feelings of inadequacy onto others, who are then criticized and demeaned for their supposed failures; for their inadequacies as a spouse in the marital relationship and for their failures and inadequacies as a parent in the custody dispute.

Spousal criticism surrounding divorce should always be met with healthy skepticism until verified in a balanced assessment, since spousal criticism may be laden with *projection* and *splitting*. Recognizing and diagnosing projection and splitting are advanced psychological skill sets requiring expertise in psychodynamic processes and personality disorder pathology. However, legal professionals who are working with potentially narcissistic or borderline parental pathology should be cognizant of both *splitting* and *projection* as potentially operative psychological processes that could be evident in the family situation. Skepticism and close consultation with mental health professionals who are skilled in the assessment of psychodynamic and personality disorder pathology is warranted.

Triangulation of the Child

There are four primary schools of psychotherapy, Psychodynamic, Cognitive-Behavioral, Humanistic-Existential, and Family Systems therapy. In high-conflict divorce, family systems constructs are vital to unraveling and resolving the complex interrelated family relationships that are creating the family's intractable conflict.

A central construct of family therapy is "triangulation" – in which a third person (the child) is brought into the spousal conflict in order to meet the emotional and psychological needs of the allied parent:

> "In the throes of their own insecurity, troubled parents may rely on the child to meet the parent's emotional needs, turning to the child to provide the parent with support, nurturance, or comforting. Ultimately, preoccupation with the parents' needs threatens to interfere with the child's ability to develop autonomy, initiative, self-reliance, and a secure internal working model of the self and others." (Kerig, 2005, p. 6)

> "By binding the child in an overly close and dependent relationship, the enmeshed parent creates a psychological unhealthy childrearing environment that interferes with the child's development of an autonomous self." (Kerig, 2005, p. 10)

The parent-child alliance that is formed by the child's triangulation into the spousal conflict is referred to as a "cross-generational coalition" of the child with one parent against the other parent:

> "The boundary between the parental subsystem and the child becomes diffuse, and the boundary around the parents-child triad, which should be diffuse, becomes inappropriately rigid. This type of structure is called a rigid triangle... The rigid triangle can also take the form of a stable coalition. One of the

parents joins the child in a rigidly bounded cross-generational coalition against the other parent." (Minuchin, 1974, p. 102)

The preeminent family systems therapist, Jay Haley, defines the construct of the cross-generational coalition as being a "perverse triangle" because it psychologically violates generational boundaries:

"The people responding to each other in the triangle are not peers, but one of them is of a different generation from the other two... In the process of their interaction together, the person of one generation forms a coalition with the person of the other generation against his peer. By 'coalition' is meant a process of joint action which is *against* the third person... The coalition between the two persons is denied. That is, there is certain behavior which indicates a coalition which, when it is queried, will be denied as a coalition... In essence, the perverse triangle is one in which the separation of generations is breached in a covert way. When this occurs as a repetitive pattern, the system will be pathological." (Haley, 1977, p. 37)

Note that the definition of a cross-generational coalition explicitly states that "there is a certain behavior which indicates a coalition which, when it is queried, will be denied as a coalition." By definition, the cross-generational coalition of the parent and child will be denied. The presence of a cross-generational coalition must therefore be determined by the features of the family relationship patterns, not from reports of the involved family members. Mental health professionals trained in family systems therapy and who are treating the entire family can make this identification. Individual child therapists will be unable to identify a cross-generational coalition because individual child therapy does not provide sufficient family-related information to identify the patterns within family relationships.

In his seminal work, *Families and Family Therapy*, the preeminent family systems therapist, Salvador Minuchin, provides a clinical example of the impact of a cross-generational coalition that occurs within a family following divorce:

"An inappropriately rigid cross-generational subsystem of mother and son versus father appears, and the boundary around this coalition of mother and son excludes the father. A cross-generational dysfunctional transactional pattern has developed." (Minuchin, 1974, p. 61-62)

"The parents were divorced six months earlier and the father is now living alone... Two of the children who were very attached to their father, now refuse any contact with him. The younger children visit their father but express great unhappiness with the situation." (Minuchin, 1974, p. 101)

Role-Reversal Relationship

The narcissistic parent will intentionally seek to establish an alliance with the child against the other parent in order to meet the emotional and psychological needs of the narcissistic parent. This is called a "role-reversal" relationship in which the child is used (manipulated and exploited) to meet the needs of the parent.

- In a healthy parent-child relationship, the *child* uses the parent to meet the *child's* emotional and psychological needs.

- In a role-reversal relationship, the **parent** uses the child to meet the **parent's** emotional and psychological needs.

A role-reversal relationship is considered a "boundary violation" of the child's psychological integrity:

"Examination of the theoretical and empirical literatures suggests that there are four distinguishable dimensions to the phenomenon of boundary dissolution: role reversal, intrusiveness, enmeshment, and spousification." (Kerig, 2005, p. 8)

Intrusive parenting is one of the characteristics of parental psychological control of the child:

"Parental psychological control is defined as verbal and nonverbal behaviors that intrude on youth's emotional and psychological autonomy." (Stone, Buehler, & Barber, 2002, p. 57)

"A second, common characterization of psychological control in the literature is that it is parenting that is intrusive. This helps clarify that psychological control is behavior that violates the child's psychological world." (Barber & Harmon, 2002, p. 15)

Psychological boundary violations are associated with the emotional and psychological abuse of the child. In the *Journal of Emotional Abuse*, Kerig states:

"The breakdown of appropriate generational boundaries between parents and children significantly increases the risk for emotional abuse." (Kerig, 2005, p. 6)

Parental Psychological Control

The construct of parental psychological control of children is extensively supported in the scientific literature. In the book, *Intrusive Parenting: How Psychological Control Affects Children and Adolescents*, published by the American Psychological Association, Brian Barber and his colleague, Elizabeth Harmon, identify and describe 40 empirically validated scientific studies demonstrating the psychological control of children by parents. According to Barber and Harmon:

"Psychological control refers to parental behaviors that are intrusive and manipulative of children's thoughts, feelings, and attachment to parents." (Barber & Harmon, 2002, p. 15)

Soenens and Vansteenkiste describe the various methods used to achieve parental psychological control of the child:

"Psychological control can be expressed through a variety of parental tactics, including (a) guilt-induction, which refers to the use of guilt inducing strategies to pressure children to comply with a parental request; (b) contingent love or love withdrawal, where parents make their attention, interest, care, and love contingent upon the children's attainment of parental standards; (c) instilling anxiety, which refers to the induction of anxiety to make children comply with parental requests; and (d) invalidation of the child's perspective, which pertains to parental constraining of the child's spontaneous expression of thoughts and feelings." (Soenens & Vansteenkiste, 2010, p. 75)

Parental psychological control of the child represents a violation of the psychological integrity of the child:

"The essential impact of psychological control of the child is to violate the self-system of the child." (Barber & Harmon: 2002, p. 24)

"The central elements of psychological control are intrusion into the child's psychological world and self-definition and parental attempts to manipulate the child's thoughts and feelings through invoking guilt, shame, and anxiety. Psychological control is distinguished from behavioral control in that the parent attempts to control, through the use of criticism, dominance, and anxiety or guilt induction, the youth's thoughts and feelings rather than the youth's behavior." (Stone, Buehler, and Barber, 2002, p. 57)

Barber and Harmon reference the established research regarding the damage that this violation of the child's psychological integrity has on the child:

"Numerous elements of the child's self-in-relation-to-parent have been discussed as being compromised by psychologically controlling behaviors such as...

Individuality (Goldin, 1969; Kurdek, et al., 1995; Litovsky & Dusek, 1985; Schaefer, 1965a, 1965b, Steinberg, Lamborn, Dornbusch, & Darling, 1992);

Individuation (Barber et al., 1994; Barber & Shagle, 1992; Costanzo & Woody, 1985; Goldin, 1969, Smetana, 1995; Steinberg & Silverberg, 1986; Wakschlag, Chase-Landsdale & Brooks-Gunn, 1996; 1996);

Independence (Grotevant & Cooper, 1986; Hein & Lewko, 1994; Steinberg et al., 1994);

Degree of psychological distance between parents and children (Barber et all, 1994);

and threatened attachment to parents (Barber, 1996; Becker, 1964)." (Barber & Harmon, 2002, p. 25)

Research by Stone, Buehler, and Barber establishes the link between parental psychological control of children and marital conflict:

"This study was conducted using two different samples of youth. The first sample consisted of youth living in Knox County, Tennessee. The second sample consisted of youth living in Ogden, Utah." (Stone, Buehler, and Barber, 2002, p. 62)

"The analyses reveal that variability in psychological control used by parents is not random but it is linked to interparental conflict, particularly covert conflict. Higher levels of covert conflict in the marital relationship heighten the likelihood that parents would use psychological control with their children. This might be because both parental psychological control and covert conflict are anxiety-driven. They share defining characteristics, particularly the qualities of intrusiveness, indirectness, and manipulation." (Stone, Buehler, and Barber, 2002, p. 86)

Stone, Buehler, and Barber offer an explanation for their finding that intrusive parental psychological control of children is related to high inter-spousal conflict:

"The concept of triangles "describes the way any three people relate to each other and involve others in emotional issues between them" (Bowen, 1989, p. 306). In the anxiety-filled environment of conflict, a third person is triangulated, either temporarily or permanently, to ease the anxious feelings of the conflicting partners. By default, that third person is exposed to an anxiety-provoking and disturbing atmosphere. For example, a child might become the scapegoat or focus of attention, thereby transferring the tension from the marital dyad to the parent-child dyad. Unresolved tension in the marital relationship might spill over to the parent-child relationship through parents' use of psychological control as a way of securing and maintaining a strong emotional alliance and level of support from the child. As a consequence, the triangulated youth might feel pressured or obliged to listen to or agree with one parents' complaints against the other. The resulting enmeshment and cross-generational coalition would exemplify parents' use of psychological control to coerce and maintain a parent-youth emotional alliance against the other parent (Haley, 1976; Minuchin, 1974)." (Stone, Buehler, and Barber, 2002, p. 86-87)

The narcissistic parent is particularly prone to exercising psychological control over the child:

"To the extent that parents are narcissistic, they are controlling, blaming, self-absorbed, intolerant of others' views, unaware of their children's needs and of the effects of their behavior on their children, and require that the children see them as the parents wish to be seen. They may also demand certain behavior from their children because they see the children as extensions of themselves, and need the children to represent them in the world in ways that meet the parents' emotional needs." (Rappoport, 2005, p. 2)

"Rather than telling the child directly what to do or think, as does the behaviorally controlling parent, the psychologically controlling parent uses indirect hints and responds with guilt induction or withdrawal of love if the child refuses to comply. In short, an intrusive parent strives to manipulate the child's thoughts and feelings in such a way that the child's psyche will conform to the parent's wishes." (Kerig, 2005, p. 12)

"In regard to narcissistic parents, the child must exhibit the same qualities, values, feelings, and behavior which the parent employs to defend his or her self-esteem." (Rappoport, 2005, p. 3)

Parental invalidation of the child's perceptions is called an *invalidating environment*:

"Invalidating environments during childhood contribute to development of emotion dysregulation; they also fail to teach the child how to label and regulate arousal, how to tolerate emotional distress, and when to trust her own emotional responses as reflections of valid interpretations of events." (Linehan, 1993, p. 42)

"In extremely invalidating environments, parents or caregivers do not teach children to discriminate effectively between what they feel and what the caregivers feel, what the child wants and what the caregiver wants (or wants the child to want), what the child thinks and what the caregiver thinks." (Fruzzetti, Shenk, & Hoffman, 2005, p. 1021)

Disregard for Truth and Authority

The narcissistic personality feels entitled to arbitrarily construct truth and reality in whatever fashion they need it to be, and they do not feel constrained by the limits of actual truth and authentic reality:

"They [narcissists] are above the rules that govern other people." (Beck et al., 2004, p. 43)

"Another conditional assumption of power is the belief of exemption from normal rules and laws, even the laws of science and nature." (Beck et al., 2004, p. 251-252)

"There is also a tendency for them [narcissists] to flout conventional rules of shared social living. Viewing reciprocal social responsibilities as being inapplicable to themselves, they show and act in a manner that indicates a disregard for matters of personal integrity, and an indifference to the rights of others." (Millon, 2011, p. 389)

"Narcissistic individuals also use power and entitlement as evidence of superiority... As a means of demonstrating their power, narcissists may alter boundaries, make unilateral decisions, control others, and determine exceptions to rules that apply to other, ordinary people." (Beck et al., 2004, p. 251)

"Thus, he or she is apt to approach any number of situations feeling automatically entitled to personal gratification." (Beck et al., 2004, p. 252)

The narcissistic parent's fundamental disregard for authority and the rights of others will lead to frequent violations of Court orders for custody and visitation, which will require that the other parent repeatedly return to Court to seek enforcement of prior Court orders.

For the narcissistic personality, truth and reality are whatever they assert them to be, irrespective of what actual truth and reality may be. This forces the other parent to spend considerable amounts of time and effort trying to defend against onslaughts of false accusations and distorted truth. The parent who is targeted by the narcissistic personality's false allegations and self-created reality may eventually begin documenting all conversations and communications with the narcissistic ex-spouse in order to establish a foundation to reality:

> "Narcissists are neither disposed to stick to objective facts or to restrict their actions within the boundaries of social custom or cooperative living... Free to wander in their private world of fiction, narcissists may lose touch with reality, lose their sense of proportion, and begin to think along peculiar and deviant lines." (Millon, 2011, p. 415)

> "Rarely physically abusive, anger among narcissists usually takes the form of oral vituperation and argumentativeness. This may be seen in a flow of irrational and caustic comments in which others are upbraided and denounced as stupid and beneath contempt. These onslaughts usually have little objective justification, are often colored by delusions, and may be directed in a wild, hit-or-miss fashion in which the narcissist lashes out at those who have failed to acknowledge the exalted status in which he or she demands to be seen." (Millon, 2011, pp. 408).

Delusional Beliefs

The level of distorted reality can reach delusional proportions, especially in response to psychological stress such as the interpersonal rejection and abandonment inherent to divorce:

> "Under conditions of unrelieved adversity and failure, narcissists may decompensate into paranoid disorders. Owing to their excessive use of fantasy mechanisms, they are disposed to misinterpret events and to construct delusional beliefs. Unwilling to accept constraints on their independence and unable to accept the viewpoints of others, narcissists may isolate themselves from the corrective effects of shared thinking. Alone, they may ruminate and weave their beliefs into a network of fanciful and totally invalid suspicions. Among narcissists,

delusions often take form after a serious challenge or setback has upset their image of superiority and omnipotence. They tend to exhibit compensatory grandiosity and jealousy delusions in which they reconstruct reality to match the image they are unable or unwilling to give up. Delusional systems may also develop as a result of having felt betrayed and humiliated. Here we may see the rapid unfolding of persecutory delusions and an arrogant grandiosity characterized by verbal attacks and bombast." (Millon, 2011, pp. 407-408).

In most social encounters we expect other people to have a basic grounding in shared truth and reality. This assumption is not warranted when dealing with a narcissistic personality:

"Were narcissists able to respect others, allow themselves to value others' opinions, or see the world through others' eyes, their tendency toward illusion and unreality might be checked or curtailed. Unfortunately, narcissists have learned to devalue others, not to trust their judgments, and to think of them as naïve and simpleminded. Thus, rather than question the correctness of their own beliefs they assume that the views of others are at fault. Hence, the more disagreement they have with others, the more convinced they are of their own superiority and the more isolated and alienated they are likely to become." (Millon, 2011, p. 415)

"Deficient in social controls and self-discipline, the tendency of CEN narcissists to fantasize and distort may speed up. The air of grandiosity may become more flagrant. They may find hidden and deprecatory meanings in the incidental behavior of others, becoming convinced of others malicious motives, claims upon them, and attempts to undo them. As their behaviors and thoughts transgress the line of reality, their alienation will mount, and they may seek to protect their phantom image of superiority more vigorously and vigilantly than ever... No longer in touch with reality, they begin to accuse others and hold them responsible for their own shame and failures. They may build a "logic" based on irrelevant and entirely circumstantial evidence and ultimately construct a delusion system to protect themselves from unbearable reality." (Millon, 2011, p. 415)

Under the distorting influence of the narcissistic parent, the child's reporting on interactions with the other parent may become similarly distorted and inaccurate, reflecting self-serving motivations to blame the other parent as "all-bad" (*splitting*) while glossing over the child's own role in provoking the parent-child conflict (externalizing blame and responsibility). Children's reporting on relationships and interactions within the family represents one source of information, but in cases of high-conflict divorce involving a potential narcissistic parent it is important to obtain balanced information from multiple perspectives.

The child who is being psychologically influenced by the distorted truth of a narcissistic parent may also begin to adopt a similar attitude of *entitlement* as is held by the allied narcissistic parent, leading the child to challenge the legitimate authority of the other parent and even the authority of Court orders. This sense of entitlement is a defining feature of the narcissistic personality:

> "Has a sense of entitlement, (i.e., unreasonable expectations of especially favorable treatment or automatic compliance with his or her expectations)." (DSM-5 Diagnostic Criteria 5; American Psychiatric Association, 2013, p. 670)

Under the psychological control of a narcissistic parent, the child may feel entitled to defy Court orders for custody and visitation and may begin refusing Court ordered visitation. In extreme cases the child may even threaten to run away from the care of the other parent in direct defiance of Court orders for visitation and custody. Normal-range and emotionally healthy children respect and cooperate with the legitimate authority of parents, teachers, therapists, and the Court. Narcissistically over-empowered children feel entitled to judge and defy adult authority, including the legitimate authority of the Court regarding custody and visitation schedules.

Trauma Reenactment Narrative

The developmental origins of narcissistic personality traits is in childhood attachment trauma:

> "Research shows that disturbances with attachment and bonding in early childhood affect personality development and healthy interpersonal functioning as an adult, often resulting in the development of personality disorders." (Trippany, Helm, & Simpson, 2006, p. 101)

> "Psychological processes that result in personality structure are endowed with a fair degree of sensitivity to the environment, especially to family environment, during the early years of life... Psychopathic personality, a consequence of development having occurred in a severely atypical family environment during the first three or so years of life, can be regarded as an example of this mode of personality maldevelopment." (Bowlby, 1973, p. 367-368)

Childhood attachment trauma is then reprocessed throughout adulthood as reenactments of the earlier relationship patterns:

> "No variables, it is held, have more far-reaching effects on personality development than have a child's experiences within his family: for, starting during the first months of his relations with his mother figure, and extending through the years of childhood and adolescence in his relations with both parents, he builds up working models of how attachment figures are likely to behave towards him in any of a variety of situations; and on those models are based all his expectations, and therefore all his plans for the rest of his life." (Bowlby, 1973, p. 369).

> "Victims of past trauma may respond to contemporary events as though the trauma has returned and re-experience the hyperarousal that accompanied the initial trauma." (Trippany, Helm, & Simpson, 2006, p. 100)

"Due to early traumatic childhood experiences, systems mediating attachment feelings and behavior have been deactivated and distorted, resulting in heightened sensitivity to separation and loss. However, because thoughts and feelings have been disconnected from the circumstances that elicited them, these individuals are not aware of why they react as they do." (Sable, 1997, p. 173)

"When the trauma fails to be integrated into the totality of a person's life experiences, the victim remains fixated on the trauma. Despite avoidance of emotional involvement, traumatic memories cannot be avoided: even when pushed out of waking consciousness, they come back in the form of reenactments, nightmares, or feelings related to the trauma... Recurrences may continue throughout life during periods of stress." (van der Kolk, 1987, p. 5)

"Viewing the client's struggles from a trauma framework allows the counselor to view the symptoms as coping mechanisms for his or her trauma history and allows for the explanation to the client, in a nonthreatening manner of how such past experiences are being reenacted through present choices." (Weniger, Lange, Sachsse, & Irle, 2009, p. 105)

The specific pattern of trauma reenactment is predictable based on the earlier childhood pattern of the abuse:

"Reenactments of the traumatic past are common in the treatment of this population and frequently represent either explicit or coded repetitions of the unprocessed trauma in an attempt at mastery. Reenactments can be expressed psychologically, relationally, and somatically and may occur with conscious intent or with little awareness. One primary transference-countertransference dynamic involves reenactment of familiar roles of victim-perpetrator-rescuer-bystander in the therapy relationship. Therapist and client play out these roles, often in complementary fashion with one another, as they relive various aspects of the client's early attachment relationships." (Pearlman & Courtois, 2005, p. 455)

The presentation to mental health and legal professionals of a false trauma reenactment pattern of "abusive parent"/"victimized child"/"protective parent" will be common with the narcissistic parent. In this trauma reenactment storyline, the other parent is falsely cast in the role as the supposedly "abusive parent" and the child is led and manipulated by the influence of the narcissistic parent into adopting the role as the supposedly "victimized child," while the narcissistic parent self-adopts and then conspicuously displays to others the coveted role as the all-wonderful "protective parent." In this false trauma reenactment narrative, the mental health or legal professional will be cast in the role as the "bystander," whose role is to validate the false storyline of "abusive parent"/"victimized child"/"protective parent" being constructed by the narcissistic pathology, and to then collude with the enactment of this false narrative by punishing the supposedly offending targeted parent for alleged parental/(spousal) inadequacies. Mental health and legal professionals working with narcissistic parental pathology must be alert for the presentation of a false trauma reenactment narrative of "abusive parent"/"victimized child"/"protective parent" that is born in the childhood attachment trauma of the narcissistic parent:

> "Trauma, as a wound that never heals, succeeds in transforming the subsequent world into its own image, secure in its capacity to re-create the experience for time immemorial. It succeeds in passing the experience from one generation to the next. The present is lived *as if* it were the past." (Prager, 2003, p. 176)

Processing Sadness & Grief

The narcissistic personality is fundamentally unable to process sadness and grief:

> "They [narcissists] are especially deficient in genuine feelings of sadness and mournful longing; their incapacity for experiencing depressive reactions is a basic feature of their personalities. When abandoned or disappointed by other people they may show what on the surface looks like depression, but which on further examination emerges as anger and resentment, loaded with revengeful wishes, rather than real sadness for the loss of a person whom they appreciated." (Kernberg, 1975p. 229)

Divorce and the loss of the intact family structure creates sadness and grief for everyone involved. Even if the marriage itself was filled with conflict, still there will be sadness and grief at its loss. However, the narcissistic personality parent is unable to process "sadness and mournful longing" and instead translates these feelings into "anger and resentment, loaded with revengeful wishes" directed toward the other spouse.

Yet because of the divorce, the narcissistic parent can no longer express their anger and "revengeful wishes" directly toward the other spouse. However, they still remain connected to their ex-spouse by their shared parenting with the child. The narcissistic parent can still express anger and "revengeful wishes" indirectly through the exploitation and psychological control of the child. The narcissistic parent will then influence the child to adopt the same feelings of anger and resentment toward the other parent as a means of expressing *spousal* anger and "revengeful wishes" toward the other *spouse*:

> "Psychological control refers to parental behaviors that are intrusive and manipulative of children's thoughts, feelings, and attachment to parents." (Barber & Harmon, 2002, p. 15)

"If others fail to satisfy the narcissist's "needs," including the need to look good, or be free from inconvenience, then others "deserve to be punished"... Even when punishing others out of intolerance or entitlement, the narcissist sees this as "a lesson they need, for their own good." (Beck, 2004, p. 252)

Under the distorting parental influence of the narcissistic parent, the child is led into adopting the same attitudes and beliefs regarding the other parent "deserving" to be punished as a "lesson they need, for their own good" for supposedly causing the divorce (through their alleged parental/spousal inadequacy):

"In a narcissistic encounter, there is, psychologically, only one person present. The co-narcissist disappears for both people, and only the narcissistic person's experience is important." (Rappoport, 2005, p. 3)

"The central elements of psychological control are intrusion into the child's psychological world and self-definition and parental attempts to manipulate the child's thoughts and feelings through invoking guilt, shame, and anxiety. Psychological control is distinguished from behavioral control in that the parent attempts to control, through the use of criticism, dominance, and anxiety or guilt induction, the youth's thoughts and feelings rather than the youth's behavior." (Stone, Buehler, and Barber, 2002, p. 57)

In normal-range and healthy relationships, parents help children understand the meaning of the child's experiences. In the role-reversal relationship with a narcissistic parent, however, the narcissistic parent distorts the meaning of the divorce for the child. The child's sadness surrounding the divorce is converted by the narcissistic parent into the same experience as the parent; i.e., as a narcissistic reflection of the parent's own experience of "anger and resentment, loaded with revengeful wishes" against the other spouse (the other parent) who supposedly "deserves" to suffer "for their own good" because of their supposed inadequacy as a spouse and parent.

"In regard to narcissistic parents, the child must exhibit the same qualities, values, feelings, and behavior which the parent employs to defend his or her self-esteem." (Rappoport, 2005, p. 3)

The Co-Narcissistic Child

The person who is in a relationship with a narcissistic personality has been referred to as a co-narcissist (Rappoport, 2005). This partner of the narcissistic personality develops a set of traits that are designed to cope with the hostile and irrational outbursts of the narcissistic personality partner by keeping the narcissistic partner in a stable and regulated emotional and psychological state. Through this set of co-narcissistic traits, the child becomes an external "regulatory object" for the narcissistic parent's internal emotional and psychological state.

As a result of this regulatory role for the parent, children of a narcissistic parent will often evidence a high degree of compliance and cooperation in order to avoid the rejection and hostility of the narcissistic parent by instead gratifying the narcissistic parent's self-perception of grandiose perfection:

> "What defines compliance in this sense is that the child becomes the counterpart of the parent's needs from moment to moment to help the parent manage threats to his or her self-esteem." (Rappoport, 2005, p. 4)

The love of a narcissistic parent is conditional on the child meeting the emotional and psychological needs of the parent. The child is under a constant threat of parental rejection if the child fails to meet the needs of the narcissistic parent:

> "The insidiously manipulative tactics used by internally controlling parents are relatively more likely to induce feelings of undue loyalty towards parents and other internal pressures to comply with parental authority. Such compliance would be driven by a desire to avoid feeling guilty and by anxiety to lose parents' love." (Soenens & Vansteenkiste, 2010, p. 82)

> "The patient with NPD [narcissistic personality disorder] often has a low tolerance for frustration and expects not only to have

wishes easily gratified but also to remain in a steady state of positive reinforcement. Conditional assumptions may include the notions, "If I want something, it is extremely important that I get it," and "I should feel happy and comfortable at all times," and "If I'm not happy, no one can be happy," and "I need to feel special to feel happy." (Beck et al, 2004, p. 252)

"Role reversal occurs when the unfulfilled abusing parent seeks dependency gratification, which is unavailable from his spouse and family, from his "parentified" child, based on his identification with the "child-victim." (Green, 1980, p. 41)

The child may also display a pseudo-maturity when interacting with other adults, which other adults may find endearing and captivating:

"Co-narcissistic people, as a result of their attempts to get along with their narcissistic parents, work hard to please others, defer to other's opinions, worry about how others think and feel about them." (Rappoport, 2005, p. 4)

"Because children of narcissistic parents may be required to fulfill their parents' needs for admiration and recognition, they may develop pleasing others' behavior in excess of children of non-narcissistic parents and may display what appears to be heightened empathic skills which may actually be hypervigilance or a heightened protective stance that masquerades as empathy." (Dutton, Denny-Keys, & Sells, 2011, p. 76)

"In order to carve out an island of safety and responsivity in an unpredictable, harsh, and depriving parent-child relationship, children of highly maladaptive parents may become precocious caretakers who are adept at reading the cues and meeting the needs of those around them. The ensuing preoccupied attachment with the parent interferes with the child's development of important ego functions, such as self organization, affect regulation, and emotional object constancy." (Kerig, 2005, p. 14)

What on the surface may appear to be a bonded relationship between the narcissistic parent and child actually represents an extremely pathological role-reversal relationship in which the child is being used (manipulated and exploited) by the narcissistic parent to meet the emotional and psychological needs of the parent. The narcissistic parent is psychologically feeding off of the child's self-structure development in order to support the inadequate narcissistic self-structure of the parent:

> "The essential impact of psychological control of the child is to violate the self-system of the child." (Barber & Harmon: 2002, p. 24). (Barber & Harmon, 2002, p. 15)

> "Narcissistic parents are seen as treating their children as extensions of themselves, expecting them to meet their own narcissistic needs, as unable to meet their children's needs for acceptance, as critical and angry when their children try to express their own feelings, will, and independent personality; and as obstructing the development of their children's true self." (Cohen, 1998, p. 199).

The Attachment System

The attachment system is a set of brain networks that manage all aspects of love and bonding across the lifespan. The attachment system functions in characteristic ways, and it dysfunctions in characteristic ways:

- All children love their parents, both parents. All children want to be loved by their parents. Both parents.

- Problematic parenting produces an *insecure attachment*. An insecure attachment <u>increases</u> children's motivation to bond to the problematic parent. Children are *more strongly* motivated to form an attachment bond to a problematic parent.

- A breach in the attachment bond of shared affection will invariably produce a grief response and a desire to reestablish the broken attachment bond of shared affection.

The attachment system evolved across millions of years of selective predation of children. Children who bonded to parents received parental protection from predators so that genes promoting children's attachment bonding to parents increased in the collective gene pool. Children who did not form an attached bond to their parents were eaten by predators or died from other environmental threats, and their genes were removed from the collective gene pool:

"The biological function of this behavior [attachment] is postulated to be protection, especially protection from predators." (Bowlby, 1980, p. 3)

"The paradoxical finding that the more punishment a juvenile receives the stronger becomes its attachment to the punishing figure, very difficult to explain on any other theory, is compatible with the view that the function of attachment behavior is protection from predators." (Bowlby, 1969, p. 226-227)

Over millions of years of evolution, a very strong and resilient primary motivational system developed that strongly promotes children's attachment bonding to parents:

> "A feature of the attachment behaviour of the greatest importance clinically, and present irrespective of the age of the individual concerned, is the intensity of the emotion that accompanies it, the kind of emotion aroused depending on how the relationship between the individual attached and the attachment figure is fairing. If it goes well, there is joy and a sense of security. If it is threatened, there is jealousy, anxiety, and anger. If broken there is grief and depression." (Bowlby, 1980, p. 4)

One of the leading figures in attachment research, Mary Ainsworth, describes the attachment system:

> "I define an 'affectional bond' as a relatively long-enduring tie in which the partner is important as a unique individual and is interchangeable with none other. In an affectional bond, there is a desire to maintain closeness to the partner. In older children and adults, that closeness may to some extent be sustained over time and distance and during absences, but nevertheless there is at least an intermittent desire to reestablish proximity and interaction, and pleasure – often joy – upon reunion. Inexplicable separation tends to cause distress, and permanent loss would cause grief." (Ainsworth, 1989, p. 711)

> "An 'attachment' is an affectional bond, and hence an attachment figure is never wholly interchangeable with or replaceable by another, even though there may be others to whom one is also attached. In attachments, as in other affectional bonds, there is a need to maintain proximity, distress upon inexplicable separation, pleasure and joy upon reunion, and grief at loss." (Ainsworth, 1989, p. 711)

Attachment bonds are not easily ended, even by severely abusive parenting. A bad parent is still better than a good predator:

> "Increased imprinting to abusing objects has been demonstrated in birds, dogs, monkeys, and human beings. Sackett et al. found that monkeys raised by an abusive mother cling to them more than average: The immediate consequence of maternal rejection

is the accentuation of proximity seeking on the part of the infant. After similar experiments, Harlow and Harlow concluded: "Instead of producing experimental neurosis we had achieved a technique for enhancing maternal attachment." (van der Kolk 1987, p. 34)

"A potential evolutionary explanation [for children's continued bonding to abusive parents] suggests selection pressures supported infants that remained attached because it increased the probability of survival. From an adaptive point of view, perhaps it is better for an altricial animal to remain attached to an abusive caregiver than receive no care." (Raineki, Moriceau, & Sullivan, 2010, p. 1143)

The attachment system is a *goal-corrected* primary motivational system, meaning that the child's attachment system always seeks the goal of forming an attached bond to the parent. Problematic parenting affects *how* the child seeks to bond with the parent, but it does not affect the primary goal of the attachment system to form an attached affectional bond to the parent. Problematic parenting increases the child's exposure to environmental dangers because of the *insecure attachment* to the parent created by the parent's problematic parenting. The insecurity of the child's attachment bond to the problematic parent acts to more strongly motivate the child to reestablish a secure and affectionate attachment bond to the problematic parent. Problematic parenting produces an *insecure attachment* bond that more strongly motivates the child to form an attachment bond to the problematic parent.

For a child to seek to cut off a relationship with a parent is extremely pathological and is evidence of severely *pathogenic parenting* (patho=pathology; genic=genesis, creation). Pathogenic parenting is the creation of significant pathology in the child through aberrant and distorted parenting practices. Either the rejected parent is extremely abusive of the child (highly pathogenic parenting by the targeted-rejected parent) or the pathogenic parenting involves the child's triangulation into the spousal conflict by the pathogenic parenting of a narcissistic parent (a cross-generational role-reversal relationship and psychological control of the child).

All children love both parents and all children want the love of both parents in return.

Child Testimony

When the child is being triangulated into the spousal conflict by the psychological control of a narcissistic parent (who forms a cross-generational coalition with the child against the other spouse/parent) the child's authenticity has been compromised:

"Psychological control refers to parental behaviors that are intrusive and manipulative of children's thoughts, feelings, and attachment to parents. These behaviors appear to be associated with disturbances in the psychoemotional boundaries between the child and parent, and hence with the development of an independent sense of self and identity." (Barber & Harmon, 2002, p. 15)

"Psychological control is defined as patterns of family interaction that intrude upon or impede the child's individuation process, or the relative degree of psychological distance a child experiences from his or her parents and family." (Barber, Olsen, & Shagle, 1994, p. 1121)

"The essential impact of psychological control of the child is to violate the self-system of the child." (Barber & Harmon: 2002, p. 24)

According to Schaefer, who introduced the construct of psychological control through his empirical research on parental behavior:

"Psychological control is suggested for this dimension, for the defining scales describe covert, psychological methods of controlling the child's activities and behaviors that would not permit the child to develop as an individual apart from the parent." (Schaefer, 1965, p. 555)

Under the influence of the psychologically controlling behavior of a narcissistic parent, the child's authenticity and independent autonomy have been compromised and lost. Under these conditions, the attitudes and opinions expressed by the child are those of the allied narcissistic parent in the cross-generational coalition:

> "In a narcissistic encounter, there is, psychologically, only one person present. The co-narcissist disappears for both people, and only the narcissistic person's experience is important." (Rappoport, 2005, p. 3)

> "In regard to narcissistic parents, the child must exhibit the same qualities, values, feelings, and behavior which the parent employs to defend his or her self-esteem." (Rappoport, 2005, p. 3)

> "In extremely invalidating environments, parents or caregivers do not teach children to discriminate effectively between what they feel and what the caregivers feel, what the child wants and what the caregiver wants (or wants the child to want), what the child thinks and what the caregiver thinks." (Fruzzetti, Shenk, & Hoffman, 2005, p. 1021)

When a narcissistic parent is triangulating the child into the spousal conflict, the child is being placed in a loyalty conflict of having to choose sides in the spousal conflict. For legal professionals to further empower the child's ability to choose sides in the spousal conflict only acts to further triangulate the child into the loyalty conflict by asking the child to choose a "preferred" parent. Asking the child to identify a preferred parent is exactly the wrong thing to do, even if the desire to designate a preferred parent appears to be coming from the child (through the hidden psychological control of the narcissistic parent). Empowering the child's ability to choose a parent will only triangulate the child further into the loyalty conflict of siding with one parent against the other parent in their inter-spousal conflict. When legal professionals empower children to choose between parents, they only expose the child more fully to the psychologically manipulative control of the narcissistic parent.

> "The need to *control* the idealized objects, to use them in attempts to manipulate and exploit the environment and to "destroy potential enemies," is linked with inordinate pride in the "possession" of these perfect objects totally dedicated to the patient." (Kernberg, 1975, p. 33)

"Psychological control refers to parental behaviors that are intrusive and manipulative of children's thoughts, feelings, and attachment to parents." (Barber & Harmon, 2002, p. 15)

"The central elements of psychological control are intrusion into the child's psychological world and self-definition and parental attempts to manipulate the child's thoughts and feelings through invoking guilt, shame, and anxiety." (Stone, Buehler, and Barber, 2002, p. 57)

"Higher levels of covert conflict in the marital relationship heighten the likelihood that parents would use psychological control with their children. This might be because both parental psychological control and covert conflict are anxiety-driven. They share defining characteristics, particularly the qualities of intrusiveness, indirectness, and manipulation." (Stone, Buehler, and Barber, 2002, p. 86)

"In short, an intrusive parent strives to manipulate the child's thoughts and feelings in such a way that the child's psyche will conform to the parent's wishes." (Kerig, 2005, p. 12)

When a child is being psychologically controlled by a narcissistic parent, the child is essentially in a hostage situation. The child is being manipulated and exploited by the psychological control of the narcissistic parent. Under these circumstances, the child's expressed attitudes and opinions are sufficiently compromised as to be of minimal to no value in determining the best interests of the child.

In cases of high inter-spousal conflict, there is a correspondingly higher risk of the child being triangulated into the spousal conflict by a narcissistic parent who coerces the child (through psychologically controlling parental manipulation) into choosing sides in the spousal conflict. Under these circumstances, the most important consideration for the child's best interests is to NOT further triangulate the child into the loyalty conflict by asking the child which parent the child prefers. Instead, the goal is to de-triangulate the child from the spousal conflict by dis-empowering the child's imposed need to select a "preferred" parent by having the adults make separate and independent decisions on behalf of the child, based on independent adult determinations regarding what represents the emotional, psychological, and developmental best interests of the child.

Whenever there is a high degree of inter-spousal conflict, children should not be allowed to testify in Court to state a preference for parents because of the considerable risk this entails of furthering the child's unhealthy triangulation into the spousal conflict by asking the child to choose between parents in the spousal conflict. Seeking the child's preference when there is high inter-spousal conflict essentially makes the child's expressed preference for a parent a "prize to be won" in the inter-spousal conflict. The child is essentially being placed in the position to judge which parent is the winner of the "best parent" award (i.e., the "preferred" parent)

The potential psychological control of the child by a narcissistic parent should always be a preeminent consideration in high-conflict divorce. Under these circumstances, balanced and objective decisions need to be made by the involved adults that free the child from having to choose sides in the inter-spousal conflict and which will consider the child's best interests from a balanced and objective viewpoint. If the Court desires that children's views should be considered, these views should be obtained by a family systems therapist who is in a balanced and objective position of interpreting the child's expressed views within a broader family context. This balanced and objective interpretation of the child's views can then be offered to the Court by the family therapist rather than by the child directly.

In order to perform their roles effectively within the potential family pathology created by a narcissistic parent, minor's counsel, guardians ad litem, and family law judiciary need to be cognizant of the potentially complex family systems dynamics involved with high-conflict divorce and the potential psychopathology of a narcissistic parent who is creating the high levels of conflict within the family. Within this context, the role of minor's counsel and guardians ad litem should be to facilitate for the Court's consideration a balanced and carefully considered analysis from professional mental health regarding the family dynamics and the child's best interests.

Epilogue: The Dark Triad

Research into personality traits has identified a pattern of three co-occurring personality traits, 1) narcissism, 2) Machiavellianism (cynical self-serving manipulation), and 3) sub-clinical psychopathy. This co-occurring set of personality traits has been called the Dark Triad (Paulhus & Williams, 2002):

> "First cited by Paulhus and Williams (2002), the Dark Triad refers to a set of three distinct but related antisocial personality traits: Machiavellianism, narcissism, and psychopathy. Each of the Dark Triad traits is associated with feelings of superiority and privilege. This, coupled with a lack of remorse and empathy, often leads individuals high in these socially malevolent traits to exploit others for their own personal gain." (Giammarco & Vernon, 2014, p. 23)

> "There is a new kid on the (personality psychology) block to rival the Big Five. The Dark Triad traits are characterized by entitlement, superiority, dominance (i.e., narcissism), glib social charm, manipulativeness (i.e., Machiavellianism), and callous social attitudes, impulsivity, and interpersonal antagonism (i.e., psychopathy)." (Jonason, Lyons, Baughman, & Vernon, 2014, p. 117)

A variation of the Dark Triad has also been identified, called the Vulnerable Dark Triad (Miller, Dir, Gentile, Wilson, Pryor, & Campbell, 2010), comprised of 1) vulnerable rather than grandiose narcissism, 2) manipulative psychopathy, and 3) borderline personality traits.

> "In the current study, we posit the existence of a second related triad - one that includes personality styles composed of both dark and emotionally vulnerable traits... The members of this putative vulnerable dark triad (VDT) would include (a) Factor 2 psychopathy, (b) vulnerable narcissism, and (c) borderline PD

(BPD)." (Miller, Dir, Gentile, Wilson, Pryor, & Campbell, 2010, p. 1530)

"We believe that the current evidence supports the existence of a second "dark" triad, one that is characterized by an antagonistic interpersonal style and emotional vulnerability... All VDT [Vulnerable Dark Triad] members manifested significant relations with similar etiological factors, such as retrospective reports of childhood abuse and colder, more invalidating parenting styles." (Miller, Dir, Gentile, Wilson, Pryor, & Campbell, 2010, p. 1554)

Professional mental health expertise in personality pathology is necessary to properly assess for the Dark Triad personality constellation, although self-report personality assessment measures have been developed to assess for the component personality traits of narcissism (e.g., Narcissistic Personality Inventory; Raskin & Hall, 1979), Machiavellianism (e.g., MACH-IV; Christie & Geis, 1970), and subclinical psychopathy (e.g., Self-Report Psychopathy Scale-III; Williams, Paulhus, & Hare, 2009). Self-report measures have also been developed to specifically assess for the Dark Triad personality constellation (e.g., Short Dark Triad (SD3) scale; Jones & Paulhus, 2014). Research on the core personality characteristics uniting the Dark Triad has also associated the Dark Triad with low scores on scale H (Honesty-Humility) on a prominent personality assessment, the HEXACO (Book, Visser, & Volk, 2015; Lee, & Ashton, 2012).

Research has linked the Dark Triad personality constellation with the absence of empathy:

Jonason, P. K. and Krause, L. (2013). The emotional deficits associated with the Dark Triad traits: Cognitive empathy, affective empathy, and alexithymia. *Personality and Individual Differences*, 55, 532–537

Wai, M. and Tiliopoulos, N. (2012). The affective and cognitive empathic nature of the dark triad of personality. *Personality and Individual Differences*, 52, 794–799

To vengefulness in romantic relationships:

Giammarco, E.A. and Vernon, P.A. (2014). Vengeance and the Dark Triad: The role of empathy and perspective taking in trait forgivingness. *Personality and Individual Differences*, 67, 23–29

Rasmussen, K.R. and Boon, S.D. (2014). Romantic revenge and the Dark Triad: A model of impellance and inhibition. *Personality and Individual Differences*, 56, 51–56

To lying, manipulative fabrication, and deception:

Jonason, P.K., Lyons, M. Baughman, H.M., and Vernon, P.A. (2014). What a tangled web we weave: The Dark Triad traits and deception. *Personality and Individual Differences*, 70, 117–119

Baughman, H.M., Jonason, P.K., Lyons, M., and Vernon, P.A. (2014). Liar liar pants on fire: Cheater strategies linked to the Dark Triad. *Personality and Individual Differences*, 71, 35–38

To attachment-related pathology:

Jonason, P.K., Lyons, M., and Bethell, E. (2014). The making of Darth Vader: Parent–child care and the Dark Triad. *Personality and Individual Differences*, 67, 30–34

And to high-conflict patterns of communication:

Horan, S.M., Guinn, T.D., and Banghart, S. (2015). Understanding relationships among the Dark Triad personality profile and romantic partners' conflict communication. *Communication Quarterly*, 63, 156-170.

Given these associations of the Dark Triad personality constellation to the pathogenic parenting of a narcissistic parent, all mental health professionals involved with the assessment, diagnosis, and treatment of parent-child relationships in high-conflict divorce should possess the requisite professional knowledge and expertise needed to assess for the Dark Triad and the Vulnerable Dark Triad personality constellations. Legal professionals seeking to evaluate the professional competence of the involved mental health professionals can examine for their knowledge of the Dark Triad personality constellation and its surrounding research literature.

References

Ainsworth, M.D.S. (1989). Attachments beyond infancy. American Psychologist, 44, 709-716.

American Psychiatric Association. (2000). Diagnostic and statistical manual of mental disorders (Revised 4th ed.). Washington, DC: Author.

American Psychiatric Association. (2013). Diagnostic and statistical manual of mental disorders (5th ed.). Washington, DC: Author.

Barber, B. K. (Ed.) (2002). Intrusive parenting: How psychological control affects children and adolescents. Washington, DC: American Psychological Association.

Barber, B. K. and Harmon, E. L. (2002). Violating the self: Parenting psychological control of children and adolescents. In B. K. Barber (Ed.), Intrusive parenting (pp. 15-52). Washington, DC: American Psychological Association.

Beck, A.T., Freeman, A., Davis, D.D., and Associates (2004). Cognitive therapy of personality disorders. (2nd edition). New York: Guilford.

Book, A., Visser, B.A., and Volk, A.A. (2015). Unpacking "evil": Claiming the core of the Dark Triad. Personality and Individual Differences 73 (2015) 29–38.

Bowlby, J. (1969). Attachment and Loss: Vol. 1. Attachment. NY: Basic Books.

Bowlby, J. (1973). Attachment and Loss: Vol. 2. Separation: Anxiety and Anger. NY: Basic Books.

Bowlby, J. (1980). Attachment and Loss: Vol. 3. Loss: Sadness and Depression. NY: Basic Books.

Cohen, O. (1998). Parental narcissism and the disengagement of the non-custodial father after divorce. Clinical Social Work Journal, 26, 195-215.

Christie, R. C., & Geis, F. L. (1970). Studies in Machiavellianism. New York: Academic Press.

Dutton, D. G., Denny-Keys, M. K., & Sells, J. R. (2011). Parental personality disorder and its effects on children: A review of current literature. Journal Of Child Custody, 8, 268-283.

Fruzzetti, A.E., Shenk, C. and Hoffman, P. (2005). Family interaction and the development of borderline personality disorder: A transactional model. Development and Psychopathology, 17, 1007-1030.

Green, A. (1980). Child maltreatment. New York: Aronson.

Haley, J. (1977). Toward a theory of pathological systems. In P. Watzlawick & J. Weakland (Eds.), The interactional view (pp. 31-48). New York: Norton.

Jones, D.N. and Paulhus, D.L. (2014). Introducing the Short Dark Triad (SD3): A Brief measure of dark personality traits. Assessment, 21, 28-41.

Kerig, P.K. (2005). Revisiting the construct of boundary dissolution: A multidimensional perspective. Journal of Emotional Abuse, 5, 5-42.

Kernberg, O.F. (1975). Borderline conditions and pathological narcissism. New York: Aronson.

Lee, K., and Ashton, M. C. (2012). The H factor of personality: Why some people are manipulative, self-entitled, materialistic, and exploitative —and why it matters for everyone. Waterloo, Canada: Wilfrid Laurier University Press.

Linehan, M. M. (1993). Cognitive-behavioral treatment of borderline personality disorder. New York, NY: Guilford.

Miller, J.D., Dir, A., Gentile, B., Wilson, L., Pryor, L.R., and Campbell, W.K. (2010). Searching for a Vulnerable Dark Triad: Comparing Factor 2 psychopathy, vulnerable narcissism, and borderline personality disorder. Journal of Personality, 78, 1529-1564.

Millon. T. (2011). Disorders of personality: Introducing a DSM/ICD spectrum from normal to abnormal. Hoboken: Wiley.

Minuchin, S. (1974). Families and family therapy. Harvard University Press.

Moor, A. and Silvern, L. (2006). Identifying pathways linking child abuse to psychological outcome: The mediating role of perceived parental failure of empathy. Journal of Emotional Abuse, 6, 91-112.

Paulhus, D. L., & Williams, K. M. (2002). The dark triad of personality: Narcissism, Machiavellianism, and psychopathy. Journal of Research in Personality, 36, 556–563.

Pearlman, C.A., Courtois, C.A. (2005). Clinical applications of the attachment framework: Relational treatment of complex trauma. Journal of Traumatic Stress, 18, 449-459.

Prager, J. (2003). Lost childhood, lost generations: the intergenerational transmission of trauma. Journal of Human Rights, 2, 173-181.

Raineki, C., Moriceau, S., Sullivan, R.M. (2010). Developing a neurobehavioral animal model of infant attachment to an abusive caregiver. Biological Psychiatry, 67, 1137-1145.

Rappoport, A. (2005). Co-narcissism: How we accommodate to narcissists parents. The Therapist, 16(2), 36–48.

Raskin, R. N. and Hall, C. S. (1981). The narcissistic personality inventory: alternative form reliability and further evidence of construct validity. Journal of Personality Assessment, 45, 159–162.

Sable, P. (1997). Attachment, detachment and borderline personality disorder. Psychotherapy: Theory, Research, Practice, Training, 34(2), 171-181.

Schaefer, E.S. (1965). A configurational analysis of children's reports of parent behavior. Journal of Consulting Psychology, 29, 552-557.

Soenens, B., & Vansteenkiste, M. (2010). A theoretical upgrade of the concept of parental psychological control: Proposing new insights on the basis of self-determination theory. Developmental Review, 30, 74–99.

Stone, G., Buehler, C., & Barber, B. K.. (2002) Interparental conflict, parental psychological control, and youth problem behaviors. In B. K. Barber (Ed.), Intrusive parenting: How psychological control affects children and adolescents. Washington, DC: American Psychological Association.

Trippany, R.L., Helm, H.M. and Simpson, L. (2006). Trauma reenactment: Rethinking borderline personality disorder when diagnosing sexual abuse survivors. Journal of Mental Health Counseling, 28, 95-110.

van der Kolk, B.A. (1987). The separation cry and the trauma response: Developmental issues in the psychobiology of attachment and separation. In B.A. van der Kolk (Ed.) Psychological Trauma (31-62). Washington, D.C.: American Psychiatric Press, Inc.

Weniger, G., Lange, C. Sachsse, U., and Irle, E. (2009). Reduced amygdala and hippocampus size in trauma-exposed women with borderline personality disorder and without posttraumatic stress disorder. Journal of Psychiatry Neuroscience, 34, 383-388.

Williams, K. M., Paulhus, D. L., & Hare, R. D. (2007). Capturing the four-factor structure of psychopathy in college students via self-report. Journal of Personality Assessment, 88, 205-219.

ABOUT THE AUTHOR

Dr. Childress is a licensed clinical psychologist currently in private practice in Claremont, California. He is the author of *An Attachment-Based Model of Parental Alienation: Foundations*, and *An Attachment-Based Model of Parental Alienation: Single Case ABAB Assessment and Remedy*. Prior to entering private practice, Dr. Childress served as the Clinical Director for a children's assessment and treatment center primarily working primarily with children in the foster care system. The clinical focus of Dr. Childress is child and family therapy, the treatment of Attention Deficit Hyperactivity Disorder (ADHD), angry and oppositional children, parent-child conflicts, parenting, and marital problems. He also has additional clinical background and expertise in early childhood mental health, with a focus on the socially mediated neurodevelopment of the brain during childhood. Dr. Childress teaches graduate level courses in Models of Psychotherapy, Assessment and Treatment Planning, Diagnosis and Psychopathology, Research Methods, and Child Development.